The Battle of Chickamauga

A Captivating Guide to the Biggest Battle Ever Fought in Georgia and Its Impact on the American Civil War

Free Bonus from Captivating History
(Available for a Limited time)

Hi History Lovers!

Now you have a chance to join our exclusive history list so you can get your first history ebook for free as well as discounts and a potential to get more history books for free! Simply visit the link below to join.

Captivatinghistory.com/ebook

Also, make sure to follow us on Facebook, Twitter and Youtube by searching for Captivating History.

Contents

Introduction

In September of 1863, the armies of the Union and Confederacy clashed along Chickamauga Creek in the northwest corner of Georgia. Rumor has it that "Chickamauga" means "river of death" in Cherokee or another Native American language. Historians have looked into this for nearly 160 years, and most of them believe this translation was likely added to the accounts of the battle for dramatic effect. After all, the Battle of Chickamauga was the second-most costly battle of the entire war in terms of casualties (men killed, wounded, and missing). Only Gettysburg, which had taken place just over two months earlier, was more costly.

The Battle of Chickamauga is a somewhat forgotten battle today. The reasons for this include the fact that over both the long- and the short-term, the battle did not decide much of anything, at least in terms of strategy or its effect on the war. The Confederate victory at Chickamauga did not turn the tide of the conflict, which so obviously had happened at Gettysburg in July, nor did it have an economic effect, such as the loss of Vicksburg, Mississippi, to the Union as the battle was beginning to take shape at Gettysburg.

Chickamauga did forestall the Union advance on Atlanta, and it did cause the Union to divert men and resources to defend the important river/rail hub at Chattanooga, Tennessee (fourteen miles to the north), but neither the battlefield nor its results had any real effect on the outcome of the war.

What the Battle of Chickamauga ultimately *did* do, however, was to further entrench and inflame both sides. Chickamauga was a costly Southern victory that only (perhaps) delayed the inevitable capture of Atlanta. It was also a humiliating Union defeat that caused the shuffling of command in that region, finally resulting in the appointment of William Tecumseh Sherman as the Union commander in the Southeast. The death toll at Chickamauga was just one more reason why the rest of the war was fought so bitterly.

Thank you for purchasing Captivating History's *Battle of Chickamauga*. We hope you enjoy reading about one of the largest battles of the American Civil War, one that has too often been overlooked.

Chapter 1 – Summer, 1863

Looking back, no one can really fault many of the Northern (Union or Federal) soldiers and civilians who began to believe the Civil War might soon be over. On July 4th, 1863, news reached most Union homes that two great victories had been won by the Federal forces at Vicksburg, Mississippi, and Gettysburg, Pennsylvania.

Union General Ulysses S. Grant had besieged the important Mississippi River port of Vicksburg for a brutal month and a half. His campaign to get to Vicksburg, which took him and his men through swamps and forests, had begun in December of the prior year. Many Northerners had almost forgotten about the campaign in the West until Grant and his second-in-command, William Tecumseh Sherman, had taken the port. With the capture of Vicksburg, Grant had seized the entire Mississippi River from the South. It was an important transport, supply, and communications highway. No one in either the North or the South could dismiss the fall of Vicksburg as inconsequential.

At Gettysburg, which lasted from July 1st to July 3rd, 1863, Confederate General Robert E. Lee had attempted to force the North to the negotiations table with a bold invasion of Pennsylvania (and perhaps even more cities if he had been successful). On Gettysburg's third day, Lee committed one of his few mistakes of the war by ordering the ill-fated "Pickett's Charge" against the distant and dug-in Union positions, costing him the battle and perhaps ultimately the war.

Still, despite these losses, the Confederacy still stood, albeit on shaky legs. Lee would retreat back to Virginia to defend his home state and Richmond, the Confederate capital city. There, for almost two more years, Lee and his men would make the Union pay for every inch of Southern ground they took on their march to Virginia.

Further south and west, the Union armies had advanced south of Vicksburg and fought the savage Battle of Shiloh, which was just over one hundred miles east of Memphis, Tennessee. The Union Army of the Tennessee under Grant then began to move south toward New Orleans (another Union force would advance from that city northward). The Union Army of the Cumberland, which was formed in October 1862 and under the command of Major General William S. Rosecrans, marched southeastward toward Chattanooga and, more distantly, Atlanta, an all-important supply and transportation hub and one of the South's largest and most important cities.

Chapter 2 – Officers and Men

Major General William S. Rosecrans

https://commons.wikimedia.org/wiki/File:GenWmSRosecrans.jpg

Leading the Union effort to seize Chattanooga and move on Atlanta was Union Major General William S. Rosecrans. Rosecrans, known to some of his peers and men as "Old Rosy," had impressed his local congressman so much that when Rosecrans was sixteen and applied to West Point, the politician bumped his own son off the West Point appointment list and gave his position to Rosecrans.

At West Point, Rosecrans was a top student, finishing fifth in his class of fifty-six in 1842, four years before the outbreak of the Mexican-American War. At West Point, he became well-acquainted with future Confederate foes James Longstreet, D. H. Hill, and Earl Van Dorn, all of whom he would meet on the battlefield at Chickamauga.

During the Mexican-American War, Rosecrans remained at West Point. He served on a variety of engineering posts around the country and resigned from the army in 1854. After this, he became a public engineer and successful inventor. However, one of his inventions, a safety lamp for mining/refining, exploded, leaving him with severe burns, some of which caused him to appear to always be grinning.

At the beginning of the Civil War, Rosecrans was in Ohio, and he was assigned by the governor to be the aide to General George McClellan, who would later gain fame and infamy on the battlefields of Virginia. Though McClellan got the credit, Rosecrans was the planner in the Union's two first victories of consequence in the summer of 1861. In 1862, Rosecrans was transferred to the Western Theater after criticizing the policies of Secretary of War Edwin Stanton, who became a lifelong political enemy.

At the victorious Battles of Iuka and Corinth, Mississippi, Rosecrans served under Ulysses S. Grant and played a major role in the Union victory at the bloody wintertime battle at Stones River, Tennessee, in 1862/63. Rosecrans was then given a corps command, which eventually became the Army of the Cumberland. He was tasked with driving the Confederates from Tennessee.

For six months, Rosecrans prepared his forces at Murfreesboro, south of Nashville, ignoring the urging of the lead Union commander in the West, Henry Halleck, and even President Abraham Lincoln. When he did move, he began a campaign that many Civil War historians rank as being up there with Grant's Vicksburg Campaign and the victory at Gettysburg. His campaign, the Tullahoma Campaign (named for a small town in central Tennessee), was more a series of carefully planned maneuvers. Rosecrans repeatedly outfoxed Confederate commander Braxton Bragg and forced him from Tennessee into Georgia, where the Battle of Chickamauga would take place.

Rosecrans's defeat at Chickamauga would forever stain the memory of his wartime career. The rest of his time in the war was spent as a military commander in Missouri, where he led troops in small actions against Confederate raiders. After the war, Rosecrans became a congressman from California, an ambassador to Mexico, and a successful businessman. He was even talked about as a potential vice-presidential candidate for Ulysses S. Grant. He died in 1898.

Braxton Bragg.

Rosecrans's chief opponent on the battlefield at Chickamauga was Confederate Major General Braxton Bragg, one of the most unpopular generals in the secessionist army. Bragg's long friendship with Confederate President Jefferson Davis allowed him to stay in command. Later on, he would become Davis's chief military adviser in Richmond.

Like Rosecrans, Bragg graduated from West Point, but he did so three years earlier, in 1837. Like Rosecrans and many other of the war's officers, Bragg met quite a few of his future opponents and comrades at the military academy. However, other than President Davis (whom he had served under with distinction in the Mexican-American War), most of his acquaintances, both in the North and the South, found Bragg to be an unpleasant and argumentative person.

In his post-war memoirs, Ulysses S. Grant tells a story about Bragg occupying two separate (and somewhat opposing) positions between the Mexican-American War and the Civil War. Bragg held the positions of both commander and quartermaster, and he argued with himself over supplies. In fact, he ended up rejecting his own requisition for supplies. His reputation for arguments, harsh discipline, and costly ineptitude would affect the upcoming clash at Chickamauga and cause noted Confederate cavalry commander Nathan Bedford Forrest to threaten Bragg's life should he attempt to give Forrest another order.

Although Bragg was victorious at Chickamauga, he was unable to retake Chattanooga. He was removed from his command to serve on Davis's staff in Richmond. He died in Galveston, Texas, in 1876, having held a number of positions in different businesses and attempting to defend his wartime career.

Rosecrans and Bragg were the overall commanders of their respective forces at Chickamauga, but, of course, their armies were organized into corps, divisions, and brigades. Many generals played a role at Chickamauga, but the most well-known today are Union General George Henry Thomas and Confederate General James Longstreet.

Thomas, a Virginian who had declared himself for the Union, would become known as the "Rock of Chickamauga" for the stout defense he led that allowed much of the Union Army to retreat peaceably to Chattanooga. Longstreet was already a famous general in the South. He was one of Robert E. Lee's righthand men in many of the famous battles in Virginia and at Gettysburg. Longstreet would be in command of the corps of Southerners that broke through the Union lines at Chickamauga and sent the bulk of Rosecrans's troops back to Chattanooga.

James Longstreet was one of the South's most respected generals. He was Robert E. Lee's righthand man at Gettysburg. (In fact, he notably warned Lee *not* to order Pickett's Charge, which may have cost the South the battle). He was a master in the use of artillery, having specialized in that branch at West Point and in the Mexican-American War. Longstreet sometimes suffered in comparison to Lee's former righthand, Thomas J. "Stonewall" Jackson, especially since Longstreet was a more cautious general. Still, despite his reputed caution (which, in reality, was simply being careful, unlike other generals in both armies who were cautious almost to the point of cowardice), Longstreet was one of the most able generals of the war.

George Henry Thomas.

https://commons.wikimedia.org/wiki/File:George_Henry_Thomas_-_Brady-Handy.jpg

James Longstreet.

All too often in Civil War histories, the lives and deeds of the soldiers of the Civil War are overlooked. While we cannot go into great detail about the lives and experiences of the soldiers at war, as this is meant to be purely an introduction on Chickamauga, we have included a number of sources in the bibliography. The American Battlefield Trust has a great site and allows you to control exactly how much information you want to absorb, from the general to the specific. Shelby Foote's *Civil War* trilogy is still one of the best sources on the Civil War, including information about the lives of the soldiers who fought. And Ken Burns's PBS series *The Civil War* is one of the best documentaries ever made, though it does contain some errors and at times appears dated, especially in the language used to describe slavery, enslaved peoples, and Confederate attitudes.

Chapter 3 – Before the Battle

Confederate General Bragg was determined to retake Chattanooga as soon as possible. Not only was the city immensely important to both sides as a rail/river and communications hub, but whoever was in possession of the city controlled a very important military position. By holding Chattanooga and the highlands around it, any occupying force had an immense advantage when it came to defense.

Aside from all the military reasons, Bragg was determined to retake the city, as it had been lost on September 9th in the most humiliating way. As was mentioned above, General Rosecrans had outmaneuvered the Southern armies outside and in Chattanooga. Bragg was forced to retreat before his forces were surrounded and besieged in the city. Though it was a necessary move to prevent disaster, Bragg's many critics (including himself) poured derision on him for being outmaneuvered and giving up the city and its environs without a major fight.

When Rosecrans occupied the city, he spent some time regrouping and resupplying before moving southeast in the direction in which Bragg had retreated. To Rosecrans, it made sense that Bragg would retreat toward the southeast to prevent an easy Union conquest of

Atlanta, which was one of the most important cities in the Confederacy.

Rosecrans was not known for being especially vain, but at a time when generals, soldiers, politicians, and civilians alike often spoke about "glory," Rosecrans chafed a bit for not receiving much credit for his truly extraordinary Tullahoma Campaign. After all, Rosecrans pushed the bulk of the Confederate forces out of central and eastern Tennessee. His campaign occurred roughly at the same time as the intense and important Battle of Gettysburg and Grant's victory at Vicksburg. Thus, Rosecrans's campaign was overlooked, and the general and many of his men wanted the nation to know that they were making great strides in the fight against the Rebels. Taking Chattanooga was a real feather in Rosecrans's cap, and if he could take Atlanta? He might become the most acclaimed general in the Union. Rosecrans did receive much acclaim for taking Chattanooga, but he was now in a position (or so he thought) to either destroy Bragg's army or force it into an endless retreat to Atlanta.

On September 9th, Rosecrans telegraphed the overall Union commander in the West, Henry Halleck, saying, "Chattanooga is ours without a struggle, and East Tennessee is free." Unlike so many Union generals had before, Rosecrans intended to move after Bragg right away and not give him the chance to regroup. He immediately sent his army south of the city and into Georgia, convinced that Bragg's forces were in disarray.

Rosecrans hoped to catch Bragg's men in a large pincer movement or even envelop the Rebel forces before he could march away. He ordered the three corps of his army to take a variety of routes into the northwestern corner of the "Peach State." General Thomas Crittenden and his XXI Corps were to follow Bragg's line of retreat. Fifty miles to the south, General Alexander McCook and his XX Corps were ordered to march as rapidly as possible. They had to move around the Southern army and cut them off from the rest of Georgia (from both reinforcements and supplies). General George Henry Thomas was initially between the other two Union forces, and he was sent southward toward the Alabama-Georgia border with the intent of eventually looping north to meet the other Union forces and cut off Bragg from his possible retreat toward Atlanta.

The problem with this strategy was that it meant that the Union forces were separated by many miles. This could affect communications and, more seriously, allow a skilled Southern general to attack each force separately. And he would have more men to do it if he could attack each group on its own.

General Thomas, who had a reputation for both being quite reserved and rarely questioning orders, suggested to Rosecrans that the Union would be better served if Rosecrans moved his army out all at once instead of dividing his forces. They would surely have the numerical advantage, and they would not have to worry as much about being outmaneuvered and outgunned. Generally speaking, Rosecrans was a conservative general, but in this case, flush with victory, he brushed aside Thomas's suggestions, believing Bragg was fleeing all the way back to Atlanta, which was just under 125 miles away. He told one of the generals on his staff that he "didn't expect to get a fight out of Bragg this side of Atlanta." He ordered Thomas to proceed.

Braxton Bragg has been rated as one of the South's worst commanders since the end of the war, and in many ways, he was— especially when you consider the "competition," which included names like Robert E. Lee and Stonewall Jackson. But he wasn't a complete loss. He was an able organizer, and like most Southern generals, he was sometimes inclined to do the unexpected, though his reputation proclaims him as being a cautious man who all too often did not press his advantage. He would rely on his cautious side after

Chickamauga, but before the battle, Bragg acted with uncharacteristic boldness.

Rosecrans believed that Bragg was in full retreat or, at the very least, would offer some resistance on the Union's drive to Atlanta. Indeed, it seemed to Rosecrans and a number of his subordinates that that was exactly what was happening. Southern prisoners told their captors that Bragg's force was panicking and on the retreat. The Union officers questioned Southern civilians, who let the Union forces believe they were tired of the conflict. They told them that the Southern officers who had slept in their homes admitted that the Confederates were panicking.

Like many commanders before and since, Rosecrans chose to believe what he *wanted* to believe. However, the truth was that the Confederate prisoners were lying. Some were actually taken prisoner in skirmishes or in the wildlands or pastures between Chattanooga and Chickamauga. They simply told the Union men what they wanted to hear. Other Southern soldiers claimed to be deserters. They weren't—they were volunteers who went into captivity with the express purpose of misleading Rosecrans and his men. Their mission was a success, and Rosecrans and many of his staff, along with many of his soldiers (who almost always want to believe what would be safest for them), fell for it. Though disheartened by the evacuation of Chattanooga, Bragg's men were not dispirited, at least not in any meaningful way, and they certainly were not disorganized and fleeing. Bragg and his corps, division, and brigade commanders worked to reorganize and resupply their men almost as soon as they left Chattanooga. Bragg's officers and men believed that their commander was going to try and do one or both of two things: move to retake Chattanooga or engage Rosecrans if he moved southeast. Shortly after the evacuation of Chattanooga, Rosecrans began to move his armies in the direction of Rome and Atlanta, Georgia, and Bragg meant to meet him sooner rather than later.

In addition to working on regrouping and resupplying his forces, Bragg asked Richmond for additional troops. In response, he was told that well-known and respected General James Longstreet would be detached from Lee's army in Virginia and sent to aid Bragg. It was Richmond's hope that Longstreet's departure would be missed by the Union, who were moving south slowly. Robert E. Lee was on the defensive in Virginia, and bad weather would be coming soon. It was also hoped that the addition of Longstreet's forces would give Bragg an advantage in numbers, which was something that the South rarely had during the war. With these numbers, Bragg could retake Chattanooga before Longstreet's men were missed in Virginia.

Rosecrans was hopeful, and for the most part, he was taken in by the misinformation fed to him by the "deserters" and locals. He also believed the reports of his scouts, who had told him that Bragg had fled Chattanooga in disarray. His successful Tullahoma Campaign had shown that he was the better field commander, and Rosecrans had begun to tell himself that his defeat of Bragg during the campaign would result in the Southerner's "panic."

Still, Rosecrans was not a fool. He had proven himself able up to that point and had served with distinction in a number of battles, including the important Corinth Campaign and in command (against Bragg) in the bloody Union victory at the Battle of Murfreesboro (also known as Stones River), which had allowed the Tullahoma Campaign to begin. On the other hand, Rosecrans was also frequently overcautious and had been within a hair's breadth of being dismissed for not moving sooner against Bragg before Stones River. Though he seemed to now believe that he had Bragg in full-scale retreat, which, in turn, made him uncharacteristically over-eager, he and his officers began to take note of the reports coming into his headquarters as his men moved east.

The area between Chattanooga and Chickamauga is marked by finger-like ridges that mostly run from the northeast to the southwest, running just over the Georgia border. In between these high ridges and hills are various coves that have few methods of easy exit and entry. The flat land just northwest of Chickamauga Creek and the town of Lafayette, the latter of which was a couple of miles to the south, consisted of sparsely populated farmland interrupted by sometimes dense woods.

As the Union troops made their way over these ridges, they began to see and hear signs of sizable Rebel forces. Contrary to the testimony of the "captured" Rebel soldiers and a number of the mountain people in the area, the Union officers began to get information from other sources, including from Washington (with which it was connected by telegraph in Chattanooga and beyond), that Bragg intended to cut them off from their supply base in Chattanooga and destroy them before reinforcements could arrive.

And this was exactly what Braxton Bragg intended to do. His plan was to force Rosecrans's army or at least a sizable portion of it into McLemore's Cove, which was pastureland surrounded on three sides by relatively dense woods. If Bragg could maneuver enough Union troops into the cove, which was a few miles to the southwest of the Chickamauga battlefield, they would likely have to surrender or be wiped out. If he could trap enough of them, Rosecrans might be forced to retreat back to Chattanooga.

Despite Union reports, Bragg's army had not gone into a panic after being evacuated from Chattanooga. Quite the opposite. Bragg, his officers, and his men were quite angry at having been outmaneuvered and were desperate for revenge. Though many of

Bragg's generals did not personally like him (as mentioned previously, he was argumentative to an amazing degree and regarded himself as a better general than he was), they knew him to be an able organizer and quartermaster. Most of his personal enemies in the Southern forces disliked him for his abrasive personality and his seeming inability to finish off an enemy when he had him on the ropes.

However, as Rosecrans's men moved into Georgia, Bragg did a number of things to ensure the Rebels were ready for them. First, he reorganized his forces. He set up a new organizational system of corps and divisions. His army would consist of four corps, with two divisions each. Bragg's corps and divisions varied in size from one another. Generally speaking, they ranged from about ten thousand to twelve thousand men to over fifteen thousand.

Bragg's corps commanders included the cantankerous Leonidas Polk, who had been an Episcopal bishop before secession and was known to many as "Bishop Polk." Polk had attended West Point, graduating in 1827, but he resigned his commission shortly thereafter. He was also the cousin of former US President James K. Polk.

There was also General D. H. (Daniel Harvey) Hill, a very able general who had transferred west after a series of arguments and disagreements with Robert E. Lee in the east. After Gettysburg, Hill was sent to Bragg, with whom he proceeded to argue as well. But, of course, Bragg argued with everyone.

General William Henry Talbot Walker was called W. H. T. Walker for the same reason that D. H. Hill was called "D. H."; there were other generals named Walker and Hill in the Confederate Army. Walker was known (as were many Confederate generals) for being hyper-aggressive, but he was extremely competent and respected by his men. Walker often led from the front and had been wounded several times before Chickamauga.

The last commander was General Simon Bolivar Buckner. He lived to be almost one hundred, and his son and namesake fought in the Pacific in WWII, commanding forces on Okinawa. Unfortunately, he lost his life in the process, making him the highest-ranking US officer to lose his life in that conflict. The original General Buckner fought with distinction in the Mexican-American War and the Civil War. He fought exclusively in the West, fighting from one side of Tennessee to the other.

These commanders would soon be joined by James Longstreet, who came from Virginia. Longstreet's journey from the east, which would cover almost 1,900 miles, would take far longer than anticipated. This was due to both the mixed gauges (width) of Southern railways (meaning that his men and all their equipment had to change trains) and the scarcity of railroad engines. Still, a sizable portion of his force, along with himself, did arrive in Georgia in time for the battle. The first group of Longstreet's men was led by General John Bell Hood, one of the South's most lauded commanders. Hill had actually been a student of Union General Thomas at West Point, but he was not the best of students. Still, on the field, Hood was an able and popular commander, despite being possibly the most aggressive and sometimes reckless Confederate general of the war. Hood would eventually command most of the Confederate troops in Tennessee, leading a sizable force on Nashville. He was also severely wounded twice: once in his right arm, which became virtually useless thereafter and had to be carried in a sling, and to his right thigh, which happened at Chickamauga and resulted in the amputation of his leg. After recovering, Hood would fight until the Confederates surrendered in 1865.

One of the advantages these commanders enjoyed was knowing where most of Rosecrans's army was, especially the southwestern force of General Thomas, which was nearing the area of McLemore's

Cove. Bragg had already moved a total of twenty-three thousand men in that direction.

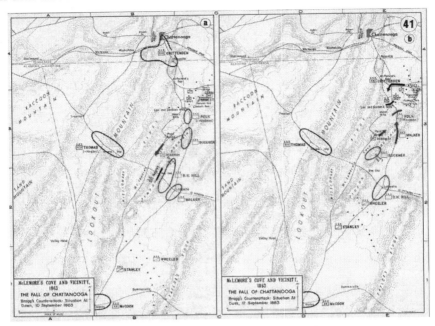

The forces of Thomas marching toward McLemore's Cove. The Southern armies cut off the eastern exits and filed in to block the north. Once Thomas entered, other CSA (Confederate States of America) forces would move south to cut off his western line of retreat. At least, that was the plan.

https://commons.wikimedia.org/wiki/File:CHICKAMAUGA_MAP_2.jpg

Throughout the run-up to the Battle of Chickamauga and the battle itself, you will see a pattern: poor communication, a rough landscape, and stubborn commanders resulted in missteps and mistakes.

Nothing about the Union move into Georgia was easy. The roads that did exist were almost all overgrown or rough dirt tracks. At times, their routes were blocked by trees cut down by the retreating Confederates. Throughout their movement east, the Rebels knew where the Union men were almost to the exact yard.

As Thomas's men moved east, Bragg gave instructions to one of Polk's division commanders, Major General Thomas C. Hindman, who had been called to join Polk's division after traveling from Arkansas. Hindman was to move into McLemore's Cove and strike Thomas's lead division. Also joining in the Confederate attack was one of D. H. Hill's divisions, which were led by noted General Patrick Cleburne, an Irish immigrant who had fought in the British Army before emigrating to the USA in 1846. Cleburne had risen from being a private in the Rebel army to division commander, and he was considered by many to be one of the South's best division commanders. Cleburne was to attack the southern part of McLemore's Cove, cutting off Negley's retreat as he was pushed in that direction by Hindman. Major General James S. Negley had led the Federal troops with skill in the Battle of Stones River (Murfreesboro) and had taken part in the Tullahoma Campaign. It was hoped that the destruction of Negley's division would cause Thomas to flood into McLemore's Cove, where Bragg could defeat him.

On September 9th, Bragg ordered Hindman to move into the cove and engage the enemy the next morning. He was to be joined by Cleburne, and together, they would destroy Negley's force. On the morning of the 10th, however, Hindman began to worry that Cleburne was being delayed for some reason or another. While his orders were to attack that morning, he began to dither, worrying that Cleburne's force would not arrive.

Hindman's gut feelings were right. D. H. Hill, Cleburne's commander, did not receive Bragg's orders for five hours. When he did receive them, Hill, who disliked Bragg intensely and who was almost as argumentative, sent out a message that was essentially a list of the reasons why Bragg's plan was a bad one. It took three hours for Cleburne's message to reach Bragg. By that time, the light was beginning to fade and, with it, Bragg's patience. By all accounts, he was pacing back and forth, occasionally cocking his ear in the direction where he intended the battle to take place. When he didn't hear any sounds, he would kick his heels into the ground and gouge out holes with his spurs.

Things didn't get any better for Bragg either. Tired of waiting for Hill's reply, he sent General Buckner and one of his divisions to aid Hindman in his attack. These two men met at 8 p.m., and after some discussion, they reached the conclusion that they would do nothing for the moment but attack some time the next day on September 11th.

Their Union counterpart in the area, General Negley, was also getting nervous. He had trailed telegraph lines along his route and signaled back to Rosecrans, saying, "There are indications of a superior force of the enemy being in position in Dug Gap [near McLemore's Cove]... My position is somewhat advanced and exposed." Negley decided that caution was the better option, and he led an organized withdrawal from the immediate area.

The next morning, Bragg decided to try again to trap a sizable Federal formation. Now it was Crittenden's XXI Corps' turn. Crittenden was moving straight from Chattanooga directly toward what would soon be the Chickamauga battlefield. Crittenden's lead division was led by General Thomas J. Wood, a West Point graduate from Kentucky who declared for the Union. This move would put him on the Chickamauga battlefield opposite his best friend, Confederate General Simon Bolivar Buckner. While Wood was moving forward, Crittenden would move the rest of his troops by rail to the small town of Ringgold, which lies a few miles southeast of Chickamauga Creek. This move put the Union troops close to Bragg's headquarters at Lafayette and a distance of fifteen miles from the rest of Crittenden's corps. If Wood came under sudden attack, no one would be able to help him and his men.

Bragg knew that there was a sizable Union force nearby and assembled the entire corps of "Bishop" Leonidas Polk to destroy it with the promise that if Polk "crushed that division...the others will be yours." Unfortunately, while Bragg knew a Union formation was in the area, he did not know *exactly* where. Polk was sent to a position that would have been ideal. Had he arrived an hour or two earlier, Wood's division would indeed have been "his," but by the time the mistake was realized, reports were already coming in saying that the rest of Crittenden's men were beginning to filter into Ringgold.

Polk was in a good position to attack a single division, but he was dangerously exposed to an attack by a greater or equally sized force. The Union corps were generally a bit larger than those of the Confederacy, of which the Confederates were well aware. The fact of the matter, however, was that Crittenden's corps was made up of three divisions, while Polk had four. Polk *did* have more men than the Union force, but he was convinced he was outnumbered. In a series of messages, Polk told Bragg he was moving back. Bragg promised him as many men as he wanted. Early in the afternoon, Polk decided to pull back rather than risk what he believed might be a disaster.

Crittenden assembled his men at Ringgold and then moved them to a more defensible position north of the town near the Lee & Gordon's Mill, where he would unite with Wood. This forced Bragg to fall back to the town of Lafayette, yelling all the while over the lost opportunity. In the years after the war, many Southern officers wrote their memoirs. The generals, in particular, often defended their moves, especially controversial ones. Bragg did this, and so did D. H. Hill and Longstreet, among others. In Hill's account, Bragg had issued "impossible orders, and therefore those entrusted with their execution got in the way [habit] of disregarding them." He also said that Bragg had a nasty habit of blaming his subordinates for his mistakes and that, consequently, they were reluctant to show initiative.

For his part, Bragg maintained that he issued clear orders that would have resulted in victory had they been followed in a timely manner.

Lee & Gordon's Mill shortly after the battle

https://commons.wikimedia.org/wiki/File:Lee_and_Gordon%27s_Mills,_Chickamauga_Battlefield,_Tenn_-_NARA_-_528904.tif

Lee and Gordon's Mill today

https://commons.wikimedia.org/wiki/File:Lee_and_Gordon%27s_Mills.jpg

Interestingly enough, at the same time that Bragg was becoming increasingly irate about his missed opportunity, Rosecrans was doing the same. Possibly because his movements in the Tullahoma Campaign had been so successful and because he had bested Bragg a number of times, Rosecrans believed that the Southern general *must* be retreating in disarray. This idea was confirmed by the false reports he was receiving from the locals and Confederate "prisoners of war." It was a classic case of confirmation bias—going into a situation or facing a problem with a certainty that is constantly confirmed because one *wishes* it to be so.

Rosecrans had actually been told by Thomas that Negley had been right in moving away from McLemore's Cove, as reports were constantly coming in reporting of large Confederate forces in the area. Rosecrans sent a message to Thomas, telling the Virginian that he had read Thomas's message carefully but was convinced that Negley had moved out of the area before he could determine the size of the force that opposed him.

Still, through the days until September 13th, Rosecrans dismissed the reports coming in. General McCook reported that "Bragg's whole army" was at Lafayette, and Negley referred to a pass in the hills near him in the aforementioned report to Rosecrans. "There are indications of a superior force of the enemy being in position near Dug Gap. My position is somewhat advanced and exposed." Later, Negley saw large clouds of dust, indicating a large enemy force.

On September 13th, Rosecrans finally acknowledged that his unit commanders might be onto something and that his corps were deployed too far apart from each other. He realized they could be cut off and destroyed before the others could come to their aid. "Old Rosy" ordered his troops back and/or together. He then ordered his corps to form a north-south line anchored near Lee & Gordon's Mill. Wood's formation, in particular, was quite a distance away and had to retrace its painful steps across Lookout Mountain. He and his troops had to march back the way they had come, a total of fifty-seven miles of hard terrain.

Thankfully for Rosecrans, Bragg was still formulating a new plan and waiting for what he believed might be the key to the battle: the arrival of James Longstreet's corps from Virginia. The long and time-consuming journey of these men from Virginia gave Rosecrans time to reassemble his troops in such a way that they could support one another in defense and deliver a devastating blow to Bragg.

Bragg was chomping at the bit to get at Rosecrans, but he was still waiting for not only Longstreet but also units under the command of Simon Bolivar Buckner, who had been sent to the area northeast of Chattanooga after its fall. He was sent there in case the Union forces did something unexpected in that direction. Bragg was also waiting on two smaller divisions from noted Confederate commander Joseph E. Johnston, which numbered about nine thousand men divided into two divisions under John C. Breckinridge (former congressman and former US vice president under James Buchanan) and General William Walker. These men had to make a long journey from Mississippi but arrived by the 13th.

As for Longstreet's troops, they were making a long circuitous 900-mile journey on different sized railways that were not in the best condition. In total, sixteen different rail lines were used, and so the Southerners often had to disembark and get on a new train.

On September 15th, Union General Halleck telegraphed Rosecrans and reported to him that Longstreet's men were heading toward Georgia. Not only were the additional numbers a threat, but Longstreet's corps was also regarded as some of the best troops on either side during the war. Halleck told Rosecrans that in response to these reports, he was sending part of Ulysses S. Grant's Army of the

Tennessee to him, as well as other troops that he could spare from other areas nearby.

One of the formations Rosecrans asked for was the Army of the Ohio, which was under the command of former overall Union commander Ambrose Burnside. He had been transferred after the dreadful US defeat at Fredericksburg, Maryland, in December 1862. Unfortunately, for Rosecrans, in this case, he, too, was the victim of his own overconfidence. Just a few days earlier, he had sent a message to Burnside, who was in northeastern Tennessee, that Bragg was in full retreat into Georgia and that Burnside could carry on with his plans to move into western Virginia. Rosecrans had asked Burnside for cavalry reinforcements to help scout the area ahead, which was done, but now with reports of Bragg seeming to be determined to make a stand, he asked Halleck to order Burnside south. But it was too late. Burnside was at Jonesboro, Tennessee, meaning he was too far away to arrive before the coming battle. He also moved slowly, which provoked President Lincoln (who followed the events on the field closely by telegraph) to exclaim, "Damn Jonesboro!" This preceded direct orders from the president to move to Rosecrans with "all haste." Burnside's men would not take part in the coming battle.

Longstreet's would.

Chapter 4 – Day One

Chickamauga was the second-most costliest battle in the entire Civil War, but as opposed to many other battles, such as Gettysburg, much of it and the events before it were accidental. As you have just read, the lead-up to the battle was marked by misinformation, misinterpretation, boldness, hesitancy, and just plain mistakes.

This was to continue until September 18th. Before we go further, remember that, generally speaking, in the Civil War, as in the Revolutionary War before it, the formations of soldiers on the battlefield were organized and lined up in ranks or rows—at least before panic set in, if it did. The first question that any student has upon learning about the Civil War for the first time is, "Why did they line up in rows like that?" The answer is quite simple. Though the weapons of the Civil War were more accurate than those of the Revolutionary War, they were largely inaccurate at any real distance over fifty or so yards. This was especially true at the beginning of the conflict. To increase accuracy and effect, troops massed together. This also allowed the individual ranks to fire, and they would then kneel to reload while the ranks behind them fired. By the time the war ended, however, technology and mass production had changed the way men fought on the field.

Since the troops typically marched in formation while on the battlefield, they had to respond to commands instantly. Today, soldiers are taught "about-face," "right-face," "left-face," and so on because it helps unit cohesion and teaches the soldiers how to respond to commands quickly and look sharp on the training ground. Militarily, it's useless today, but in 1863, the men needed to learn these commands and respond quickly while under fire. This was made more difficult, obviously, due to the sounds of battle. For centuries, men had used drums, flags, and horns to relay orders over the din of battle and over distances. It was the same in 1863, although sadly, many of the drummer boys were actually boys. Many of them suffered greatly or lost their lives in the war.

When the two opposing formations were facing each other, they referred to the ends of their positions or the position of their enemies by using the terms "right" and "left." For instance, at Chickamauga, the westward-facing Rebels' "right" was, generally speaking, northward, while their "left" was to the south. Obviously, this was the opposite for the Union. When writers or textbooks describe the battles of the era, they use phrases like "turn the enemy right" or "attack the enemy left." When the phrase "turn" is used, that usually refers to an attack on an enemy formation's flanks (the ends of the formation). It was hoped that they could force the enemy to "turn" part or all of their formation to meet the attack. In doing so, disorganization could set into undisciplined and/or badly trained troops. It could also leave a gap between the "turned" unit and its fellow unit next to it. This, in turn, could be exploited in a number of ways by the attacker.

Early on the morning of Tuesday, September 18th, Braxton Bragg was still fuming over his missed opportunities of the day before and sought to redeem them by attacking that morning. He planned to attack the forces of Union General Crittenden on the south end of the Union lines and "turn" his left flank, which would force the Union men to turn and face them on an east-west axis north of McLemore's Cove. Bragg's men would force them into the cove, where strong Confederate forces barred most exits, catching them in what Bragg called a "meat grinder." Bragg's orders to his army were clear: "The movement will be executed with the utmost promptness, vigor and persistence." In today's parlance, that would be "attack on schedule, press it, and don't lose contact with the enemy." But imagine it said with a bit of anger, as Bragg had smoke coming out of his ears due to the day before.

On the Confederate right was General Bushrod Johnson, who actually was born and raised in the North as a pacifist Quaker but rebelled and entered West Point. He had fought since the beginning of the war, beginning in the Tennessee Militia as a colonel and fighting through its end. Johnson and his troops, which were were on the far Confederate right, were to turn the Union left at Reed's Bridge over Chickamauga Creek. To his south (left), the Rebel forces under Walker and Buckner were to advance in the center and left, respectively.

Like it had the day before, fate had other ideas about Bragg's plans. Johnson initially marched in the wrong direction and had to retrace his steps, which wasted valuable time. To his south, Generals Walker and Buckner began their march to the creek, but they were miles from it. At one point, they were forced to share the same badly worn dirt road, again wasting time. General Buckner met the Union pickets (small forces sent out to prevent surprise attacks) and quickly defeated them. He waited for word of General Walker's actions, and after waiting through the afternoon, he set up camp for the night.

Both Walker and Johnson, who were to his north, were engaged with Union troops. As the Confederates approached Reed's Bridge, they met stiff resistance from Irish-born and raised cavalry Colonel H. G. Minty. He and his men fought Johnson's forces to a standstill on the narrow road. At Alexander Bridge to the south, Walker was met by the forces of another Union cavalry unit, one with a reputation for battle and surprise. It was commanded by Colonel John Wilder, and it was known as the "Lightning Brigade" for its swift movement and its ability to be seemingly at more than one place at a time. Though the Confederates eventually seized the bridge when Wilder's smaller unit retreated, it took them time to get over the bridge, for Wilder's men had removed the planking before they left. Meeting the Union cavalry in battle at Chickamauga and thereafter would not be something that many Southern units looked forward to. The Union horsemen were beginning to receive weapons that incorporated a new technology: repeating rifles. Depending on the make, these rifles could fire five or six bullets for every one fired by the Southerners.

By the afternoon, Bragg had only about nine thousand men across Chickamauga Creek. His forces, including those from Longstreet, which began to arrive in the late afternoon on the 18th, would eventually number sixty-five thousand for the coming battle. It was one of the few times in the war that the Confederates would have more men on the field than the "Yankees."

Longstreet's unit that arrived in the late afternoon was Hood's. Hood had been forced to take a different train than his men and had not seen his men since the Battle of Gettysburg in early July. There was a short, happy reunion, as Hood was immensely popular with his men. Then he led them into battle at Reed's Bridge, brushing aside the Union cavalry under Minty. The Southerners now began to send the rest of their army across the creek, and by dawn on the 19th, had about 75 percent of their forces over the water.

Chickamauga Creek and Reeds bridge.

On the Union side, Rosecrans was also busy. He had ordered Crittenden to spread his units more to the north (the Union "right") and ordered Thomas to take his XIV Corps northward. By sunrise, two of Thomas's divisions (commanded by Generals John Brannan and Absalom Baird) were in position, and two more (under James Negley and John Reynolds) were moving to the north.

However, despite their successful movements and a number of large skirmishes, both commanders had serious misapprehensions about the position of the enemy's forces. Rosecrans did not know that Bragg's men had crossed the creek, which was more like a small river. Bragg believed that the Union right was still three miles to the south. The movement of the Union troops during the day and evening meant that Bragg's planned flank attack for the 19th would not engage the Union right but move straight into the center of the Union lines.

The first truly heavy fighting in the Battle of Chickamauga took place by accident. At about 9 a.m. on September 19th, Colonel Dan McCook, the brother of Alexander McCook, the Union commander of the XX Corps, reported to General Thomas that a brigade-sized enemy force had crossed the creek in the area of Reed's Bridge. Thomas ordered General Brannan, the commander of the 3rd Division of the XIV Corps, to find, attack, and preferably capture this Rebel unit. That was easier said than done, of course, and in this case, that was doubly true. This Confederate force was the cavalry brigade of Brigadier General Nathan Bedford Forrest, who had already established himself as one of the best and most aggressive of the Confederate cavalry commanders.

Today, Forrest is a controversial figure, especially in Tennessee. His bust was removed in July 2021 from the Tennessee State House and moved to a museum. There was also a tremendously ugly statue of him erected on private land near a major highway approaching Nashville. This was removed in December 2021 (it is perhaps safe to say that even Forrest would have approved of this move). Forrest was a millionaire before the war at a time when being a millionaire was an almost unheard-of thing. He had made his fortune trading slaves, and when the war broke out, he enlisted as a private. But he soon wearied of the incompetence of his commanders. He then outfitted a unit completely on his own, and in a short time, he had established himself as an excellent military leader with an incredible feel for the battlefield. He was soon promoted all the way to the rank of general. After the Battle of Chickamauga, he would curse and threaten Braxton Bragg for his incompetence and go on to wage a brilliant campaign throughout Tennessee.

Thomas had sent a division after Forrest's brigade, and while Forrest was fighting a holding action against this larger force, he sent for reinforcements from General Walker's two-division corps, which was positioned to his south. Walker's men took McCook's men completely by surprise when they attacked the Federals' flank. The officer in charge of that attack had one of the most unique names of the war: States Rights Gist. No, that was not a nickname. His father was a staunch secessionist, going all the way back to the secession crisis of 1833 under President Jackson when South Carolina, Gist's home, threatened to leave the Union.

Bragg received a message from the field and decided that the Federal move was an attempt to turn his right flank. It was not, but Bragg began to order more units to the north part of his line (the Confederate "right" and Union "left").

Commanding the lead brigade of the Union division was Colonel John Croxton, who, while being pushed back now by both Forrest and Gist, wryly sent back a message to Thomas reporting the presence of *two* Confederate brigades near Reed's Bridge. "Which brigade should I capture?" The Battle of Chickamauga had begun almost completely by accident, and now both commanders (Bragg and Rosecrans), as well as their field commanders, were forced to improvise on the fly.

General Brannan hurried his division to the aid of Colonel Croxton and was soon involved in heavy fighting with Gist's division and Forrest's brigade. Soon after arriving on the field, Brannan was forced to give ground against a fierce Rebel attack. General Thomas, who was not far from the fighting, then ordered the 1st Division of his corps under General Absalom Baird to aid Brannan and Croxton. Soon, the Union lines steadied, and Croxton pulled his men back to resupply ammunition.

The Union line would only hold for a short time, for Bragg had ordered yet another division to his right to reinforce those already involved in the fighting. This division was led by General St. John Liddell, a Louisianan who later advocated for the emancipation of the enslaved people of the South in order to secure British aid. After the war, Liddell was killed in a duel with another former Confederate officer. The addition of Liddell's brigade pushed the Union men all the way back to their jumping-off point, and it also resulted in the capture of a small number of Federal cannons. The capture of the guns came at a high cost. The Union artillery commander, who stood alone with his men after the infantry meant to protect him fled, fired sixty-four rounds of canister shot into the coming Rebels of the 8th Arkansas Brigade. For those of you unfamiliar with the term, "canister" was essentially a cannon-sized shotgun shell. The Rebels that made it to the Union guns would have seen their comrades ripped apart before their eyes. Other Confederate units would capture dozens of Federal guns and mountains of ammunition and other supplies once the Federal right began to crumble later in the day.

Much of the fighting at Chickamauga took place in heavily wooded areas that were interrupted by various sized farms and pastures. Both types of terrain led to heavy casualties, but the heavy woods hindered both commanding officers and their men from knowing what was going on, not only in the battle as a whole but also on the ground. On many occasions, especially as the light began to fade later in the day, soldiers from both sides would be surprised by additional enemy units seeming to appear "out of nowhere." This, as well as the number of men involved in the battle, would lead to the extremely high casualty rate at Chickamauga.

While the fighting was going on at the far end of the Union left, Thomas sent messages to Rosecrans, reporting what was happening and asking for reinforcements. Rosecrans sent the 2nd Division of McCook's XX Corps—men from Ohio, Indiana, Illinois, and Pennsylvania—to aid Brannan's and Baird's men. As the men from those units retreated in some disorder from the fighting, the men of the 2nd moved onto the edges of the road to let them pass. And then, undaunted, they marched into battle and began to push the Rebels back once more.

By this time, the battle was taking on a life of its own. Bragg sent more of his men to his right. This unit, led by respected commander Benjamin Cheatham, an upper-class Tennessean by birth who had relocated to California to take part in the Gold Rush for a time, entered the fray in the mid-morning. The fighting became exceedingly heavy and hard.

Forrest's cavalry was still involved in the fighting; they had been fighting on foot for about three hours when noon approached. One of Forrest's officers, Colonel Thomas Berry, later put his impressions of the battle to paper. "Neighing horses, wild and frightened, were running in every direction; whistling, seething, crackling bullets, the piercing, screaming fragments of shells, the whirring sound of shrapnel and the savage shower of canister, mingling with the fierce answering yells of defiance all united in one horrible sound." He left out the screaming, moaning, and crying of his own men but added that he had never seen, throughout his two years at war, a more terrible sight than this. "The ghastly, mangled dead and horribly wounded strewed the earth for over half a mile up and down the river banks." Chickamauga Creek had lived up to its name, he said. "It ran red with blood." Just to be clear, this last statement was not an exaggeration. The creek literally turned red with blood.

Union commander Rosecrans was out of touch with things at his headquarters, which was at the far right of the Union line, south of Lee & Gordon's Mill at Crawford Springs. More specifically, his headquarters was located in the home of a young widow named Eliza Glenn. This position was behind Thomas's right flank and closer to the battle, but Rosecrans still did not have a clear idea of what was going on. The confusion of battle and the heavy woods in the area muddied up the picture, but as in many battles before and after, the sound of heavy firing gave Rosecrans an indication of the direction and severity of the fighting. Even though telegraph lines connected Rosecrans with Thomas, the latter was too busy issuing orders of his own to give Rosecrans an exact and detailed update. Rosecrans was even more in the dark because his maps of the area were quite primitive and did not reveal many of the features of the area. So, while Rosecrans was attempting to get a clear picture of the battlefield, the battlefield kept inching closer to him, with both sides feeding more troops into the fighting on the Union left/Confederate right. Both sides had moved forward and back. At about the time Rosecrans was approaching the Widow Glenn's (he might have already been there by this time), Union troops under General Richard Johnson were attacking Cheatham's men and threatening to open a hole in the Confederate line that other Union troops could exploit. They could possibly turn the battle their way once and for all. One of Johnson's men, a Sergeant Young of the 79th Illinois, gave a frightful account of what he saw on the battlefield that day. "Men cheer, but in that awful roar the voice of a man cannot be heard 10 feet away. Men fall to the right and left. The line stumbles over corpses as it hurries on. There are flashes in the smoke cloud, terrible explosions in the air, and men are stepped on or leaped over as they throw up their arms and fall upon the grass and scream in the agony of mortal wounds."

Now it was Bragg's turn to reinforce, and he sent the division of Tennessean Alexander P. Stewart, who, at the end of the war, would be the last commander of the Confederate forces in the West. As his men moved forward into position on Cheatham's left, some of them saw one of their comrades from Cheatham's unit being carried on a stretcher with a mortal wound. His intestines were literally hanging from his body as he cheered his brothers-in-arms on. "Boys, when I left, we were driving 'em!" This was at about 2:30 in the afternoon. Stewart's division began a short but murderous fight with a Union division under Brigadier General Horatio Van Cleve and sent it back toward the Brotherton farmhouse on Lafayette Road. In that short but brutal fight, one of Stewart's brigades, which numbered about 1,800 men, lost one-third of its men in just minutes—604 men were killed and wounded.

As Stewart was attacking, Thomas's call to his divisions under Negley and Reynolds was answered. These units were moving to the rear of Van Cleve's soldiers when it was attacked by the men in gray (and butternut) uniforms. Reynolds turned his men and came to Van Cleve's aid while Negley's men waited in the rear as a reserve. If they were not needed, they would continue their march toward Thomas.

The entry of Reynold's division was timely and accidental at the same time. It was also key; had the Confederates broken through, they would have cut the battlefield in two and moved forward to cut Dry Valley Road, which led to Chattanooga. This would have prevented any Union moves from or to that direction.

Van Cleve's men rallied alongside Reynold's before Dry Valley Road. They barely had time to catch their breath and take a quick drink before Stewart's men came roaring forward at them once again. The bloody fight continued for some time before the Union men began to fall back in a relatively orderly fashion to the north. This was the start of Thomas's stand in the area, and as troops arrived, he calmly arranged them in a horseshoe shape. During all of this, Bragg was feeding his men into the battle piece by piece. He still believed that the Yankees would try to attack and turn his left, so he kept units in place there until he needed them. This was something he was roundly criticized for during and after the war. While he was doing this, General Hood's Texans went against the Union right, which was south of Thomas on Lafayette Road. (The general had commanded the Texans personally throughout the war until taking command of

Longstreet's corps until he arrived from Virginia, which he would do the next day.)

As a unit of tired, ragged, and wounded Tennesseans came toward the rear from the front lines, one cocky Texan exclaimed, "Rise up, Tennesseans, and see the men from Texas go in!" A bit later, after having been repulsed for the time being by a unit of Union cavalry, the Texans moved to the rear, where the Tennesseans were waiting. One man stood up and said, "Rise up, Tennesseans, and see the Texans COME OUT!"

Hood's troops went in again. This time, they met the Union division under Brigadier General Jefferson C. Davis. Yes, you read right. The President of the Confederacy was Jefferson F. Davis, and he was safe in Richmond while the battle wore on. Davis's two brigades were in an unfortunate position. As the Union troops shifted from south to north, Davis's men were momentarily left with both flanks exposed. Hood's men, along with Johnson's men, inflicted heavy losses on the Union soldiers. Six hundred ninety-six were killed, wounded, or captured.

One of the men who was killed was brigade commander Hans Christian Heg, a Norwegian immigrant. A sizable percentage of the troops from both sides were immigrants. Most were Irish, but sizable contingents of Germans, Slovaks, English, Italians, and other European immigrants were fighting for their new country. Hood and Johnson began to approach Rosecrans's headquarters at the Widow Glenn's. The fighting got so close that the men in and around the building had to shout to make themselves heard. As you have read, the fighting at Chickamauga was one of attack and counterattack. So, when Hood's and Johnson's men surged forward, they were met by Union troops commanded by the unhorsed cavalry of Wilder's Lightning Brigade, who had begun the day's fighting on the north end of the Union line. Wilder's horsemen were joined by an artillery unit commanded by a man whose last name is still well-known today: chemist Eli Lilly, who began what is today the pharmaceutical giant that bears his name. Lilly set up his guns so that they faced the left flank of Johnson's men as they moved forward. Within minutes, scores of Confederate soldiers were dead or horribly wounded on the field. General Wilder blanched at the carnage and later wrote that he "had it in his heart to order the firing to cease, to end the awful sight."

By mid-afternoon, only two Union formations had not seen battle: General Gordon Granger's Reserve Corps, which was far to the north of the battlefield guarding the approach from that direction, and the division under General Philip Sheridan. Sheridan had already proved himself in battle, and he would go on to be Ulysses S. Grant's chief cavalry commander in Virginia shortly after Chickamauga. He did, however, have a bit of an inflated attitude about himself and his unit. This attitude spread to his staff officers, who cried out to other officers and men on the road to the field, "Make way for Sheridan! Make way for Sheridan!" as Sherman's division moved into position at the end of the Union line. They acted as if he was going to rescue the entire Union Army.

As his men moved into position, they were attacked by Hood's and Johnson's troops. Sheridan's defense was hindered by the savagery of the attack and the many Union troops fleeing the field, which slowed Sheridan's advance. Shortly after arriving on the field, Sheridan's unit was forced to retreat with haste. As they did, Union troops in the rear, who had watched Sheridan's grand entrance, exclaimed, "Make way for Sheridan! Make way for Sheridan!" There were comedians on both sides.

At the Federal headquarters, General Rosecrans was beginning to lose his cool. As the fighting raged nearby, a young Southern prisoner was brought to him. The prisoner told the general proudly that he was with Longstreet's corps. Rosecrans was notorious for receiving bad news poorly, and now that it seemed that even more Confederates were at Chickamauga than he had imagined, he lost his cool. He yelled and screamed in the face of the young prisoner, who quickly clammed up out of fear, believing he might be shot. Eventually, the Union commander calmed down, and as the boy was taken away, Rosecrans admitted that the youngster was probably right.

By this time, the sun was going down, and many men believed the fighting was done for the day. On the north flank of the Union forces, General Thomas began to reorganize his troops and set up a defense in the woods along the intersection of Alexander Bridge Road and Lafayette Road. Soon, this area, previously known as "Snodgrass Hill," would take on a new name based on the excellent defensive position of the troops there: Horseshoe Ridge.

As twilight fell, the men of Patrick Cleburne's division, which had been moving northward for some time from its position near Lee & Gordon's Mill, struck Thomas's position after crossing a freezing cold but only shoulder-deep ford of the Chickamauga Creek. The Southerners, mostly men from Alabama, Arkansas, Mississippi, and Texas, with a smattering of units from Tennessee, Louisiana, and Florida, unleashed a massive wall of fire at the Union lines. Cleburne had insisted on his men learning to fire rapidly, and the result was an almost continuous wall of fire. This also had the effect of making the Union men in blue believe there were many more Rebels than there actually were.

Soon, Cleburne's men and his artillery fire were pushing the Union troops rearward. One of the units in the Union front line, the 77th Pennsylvania, virtually disappeared in the initial assault. As the Rebels moved forward in the dark, they began to yip and howl the infamous "Rebel yell." In the growing darkness, lit by the firing of the guns of both sides, the fighting became hand-to-hand. Cleburne's men pushed the Union line back a mile, capturing a number of guns in the process. Their advance stopped when it became too dark to see.

It was cold. Cleburne's men were freezing from the water and sweat. The fading of adrenaline also caused chills on both sides. Obviously, no fires could be lit. As dark as it was, picket troops on both sides, who were guarding against a possible surprise attack in the night, fired at each other often, waking those who could sleep and alarming those still awake. The soldiers on both sides also had to listen to the screams, cries, and moans of the wounded and dying all around them. No one could get up and help them. When they tried, rifle and even cannon fire burst out again.

General Thomas did not sleep either, at least not very much, nor did many of his men. During the night, the Union lines were reorganized into a coherent, connected wall of blue uniforms. By morning, a high percentage of the sixty thousand Union troops at Chickamauga were at Horseshoe Ridge. The remainder formed a line of corps and divisions aligned (roughly) east to west.

The approach toward Horseshoe Ridge today.

That night, Rosecrans called a war council at the Widow Glenn's house, which would burn to the ground the next day. Philip Sheridan recalled a depressing atmosphere. Rosecrans and the others knew that they had barely managed to hold back the Rebels that day and that the Southerners were preparing a massive assault for tomorrow. Not helping matters was the realization that the Confederates outnumbered them by a sizable margin. A Union attack was out of the question, but a strong defense would reduce the Rebels' advantage.

During the meeting, General Thomas occasionally nodded off, as he was exhausted after the long, bloody day. Thomas, who was known for being rather reserved anyway, was asked throughout the meeting for his recommendation. Each time, he would open his eyes for a moment, say, "I would strengthen the left," then go back to his light sleep.

The Confederates also had a meeting. General Hood, who was new to the Western Theater, noticed both a lack of formality and enthusiasm. The latter was especially true when General Bragg announced that he was reorganizing his command. The Southern right would be made up of Polk, Hill, and Walker. On the left would be Hood, Buckner, and the soon-to-arrive General Longstreet.

Longstreet had actually arrived at 2 o'clock in the afternoon, but when he got to the nearest depot, no one was there to greet him, brief him on the situation, or even tell him how to find General Bragg. Longstreet's horse hadn't arrived yet either, and until it did, the general paced back and forth at the depot, growing more frustrated by the moment. Finally, his horse and those of his staff arrived, and they decided to follow the sound of the distant battle, questioning soldiers along the way.

It took Longstreet until 11 p.m. to find Bragg, who was some twenty miles away. By the time Longstreet and his men found Bragg, they were already convinced of the rumors about the general's "unpleasantness" and had gradually worked themselves up against him as they traveled. When they arrived, Bragg had to be woken up, and he spent the next hour briefing Longstreet on the disposition of the troops and the plan for the coming day.

Bragg's plan for the next day was similar to that of the day before: he would order his right to swing south and push the Union right south into McLemore's Cove, where they would be forced to surrender or be annihilated. From the north of his position southward, each of the units on his right flank would swing south (to their left) as the Union was pushed into that direction.

In order to do that, many Southern formations would be repositioned northward during the night, with the attack beginning at first light. At least that was the plan. D. H. Hill's division of Polk's corps was supposed to move from the far Confederate left all the way north to the Rebel far right. This never happened because Hill never got Bragg's orders. He had not been at the meeting, and Polk did not relay the orders. The "Bishop" believed that Bragg would send word to Hill, which never happened.

Hill only learned about Bragg's plans the next morning—at about the time the attack was set to begin. His men were tired from the day before and had not yet eaten. When Hill got the orders to move, he sent word to Polk that he would attack in about an hour—*after* his men had their breakfast.

Polk did not send word to Bragg, who was pacing and swearing at his headquarters some miles away. Many Southerners criticized him for being away from the action, as they expected their generals to be near the front, like Lee and Jackson.

Bragg sent a man to Polk to find out what was happening. His courier returned to report that Polk was reading a newspaper in his tent and waiting on his breakfast. At that point, Bragg finally exploded, cursing in a most ungentlemanly manner about his generals and their incompetence. He then sent a very emphatic order to his officers to attack *immediately.*

Chapter 5 – Day Two

The battle resumed at 9:45, a good three hours after Bragg had intended. All along the line, the firing of rifles and cannons began to increase and move south until the entire line was aflame.

The Union left was attacked by three brigades under the overall command of General Breckinridge, the former US vice president. Two of those units moved around the end of the Union line and attacked the regiments of James Negley, whose lead brigade was forced back behind the Union left. This began the real horseshoe shape that would define the Union position on the far north of the battlefield.

One of Breckenridge's brigades had named itself the "Orphan Brigade." They were Kentuckians, whose state was completely under Union control. As long as the war went badly for the South, they could never return to their home state, hence their name. This unit was led by a man known personally to President Abraham Lincoln. Confederate Brigadier General Benjamin Hardin Helm was Mary Todd Lincoln's brother-in-law, and the president was quite fond of the West Point and Harvard graduate.

After the battle, Private John Green of the Orphan Brigade described the fighting that took place when his brigade engaged Thomas's lines. The Orphans were "giving and taking death blows which could only last but a few minutes without utter annihilation." Indeed, Mary Lincoln's brother-in-law was cut down, sadly and ironically, by the Union 15th Kentucky Brigade. Before the war, Kentucky, though a slave state, was divided almost in half between Union and Confederate sympathies, as was Tennessee. However, most pro-Union Tennesseans were in the rugged mountains of the far eastern quarter of the state. Interestingly, Delaware and Maryland, which were both Union states, were also slave states, which many do not know.

The final two brigades of Negley's division never made it to the far left of the Union line. They were farther south in the Union center, awaiting the arrival of General Thomas J. Wood. His division was still in reserve, despite receiving orders from Rosecrans to move into the front lines where Negley's two divisions were so that they could reunite with their comrades fighting on the left flank. When informed of this, General Rosecrans rode to Wood's position and let him have it quite publicly. "What is the meaning of this, sir? You have disobeyed my specific orders! By your damnable negligence you have endangered this entire army, and by God, I will not tolerate it! Move your division at once, as I have instructed, or the consequences will not be pleasant for yourself!" Rosecrans did not have time to couch his language, but he should not have delivered his rebuke in front of Wood's men. Still, it did result in Wood moving his troops into line and into the battle. Negley's men also joined their brother units on the left.

Another Confederate division, this one under Cleburne, assaulted the Union front south after Breckinridge's attack. As they advanced through the woods, they ran into log breastworks the Union men had cut down during the night. The fighting was intense and stopped Cleburne's attack. The Rebels then settled down behind whatever cover they could find and held on until General Polk sent Walker's and Cheatham's divisions to their aid. This time, all three units attacked the Union line, and all three were thrown back, suffering heavy losses.

At about this time, something crucial to the outcome of the battle occurred. General Thomas, who was under heavy pressure, was sending requests for reinforcements every few minutes. One of Rosecrans's men, Captain Kellogg, was traveling to survey Thomas's situation in the north, riding just behind the front line to do so. On the way, he noticed what he believed was a gap in the Union lines, which had been caused by a unit presumably sent to reinforce Thomas. When he arrived at General Thomas's headquarters, he reported the dangerous situation to the general, who telegraphed it back to Rosecrans's headquarters.

This supposed gap in the lines was between the units of General Reynolds (to the north) and General Wood's division, which was now in place near the center of the Union line. Rosecrans sent a message to Wood, ordering him to move his division to the north alongside Reynolds's men and close up the hole in the Federal lines. General Wood did not understand the order; there was no gap in the Union lines as far as he could see. But he had just received a stinging public rebuke and possible court-martial from Rosecrans not too long before, so he moved his unit as ordered. This created a division-sized gap in the Union lines.

At about 11:30 a.m., Rosecrans ordered the Union's Jefferson Davis into Wood's former position to the south. While this was happening, two of Philip Sheridan's brigades were sent north from the south of the "gap" to Thomas in the north. At this point in time, two Union divisions and half of another were in motion, moving sideways to the front, which created a gap a quarter-mile wide in the Union lines. There was no gap before—it was part of the "fog of war"—but there was one now.

Chickamauga was a strange battle in a number of ways. Many of the actions took place by accident or misunderstanding, and this situation was no different. Shortly after the Northern units began their shift northward, the Confederates under James Longstreet, who had finally made it to the front lines after his long journey, launched a massive attack at exactly where Wood's unit had pulled out. Three divisions (Hood and Johnson in front, with Brigadier General Joseph B. Kershaw in reserve) went charging into the gap in the Union lines. This was a total of twenty-three thousand men.

Though they took heavy losses from Union artillerymen, some of which actually threw pieces of grapeshot (chains, nails, etc.) by hand at the Rebels, the Southern men surged forward. They engaged in hand-to-hand fighting with the two batteries of Union artillery and moved on into a clearing near Dyer Farm to recoup and catch their breath.

At this point, General Hood rode up, using his one good arm to ride and ordering Johnson forward. Soon after, the Rebel yell went up, and the entire line of Southerners advanced over abandoned Union breastworks and into the fields beyond. Both Johnson's and Hood's divisions were moving forward when a surprise attack by a hidden Union brigade began. One Union rifleman struck a key target, that of General Hood, who took a .50 caliber Minié ball (a primitive bullet) in the upper thigh of his right leg, breaking his femur, which is one of the most painful places for a break. When he fell off his horse, the men from his old Texas Brigade caught him. Orderlies brought him to the rear, where his leg was eventually amputated, and his division, along with Johnson's and Kershaw's men, surged forward.

To the left of Hood's position was Confederate Major General Thomas Hindman, who was also pushing forward. All of this combined to begin a rout of the Union forces on the front lines. Davis's men began to fall back, and they eventually panicked and fled to the rear. As they did so, they ran head-on into Sheridan's division, causing that unit to become disorganized and eventually panic themselves. One can only imagine the cries that went out toward Sheridan's men: "Run! Save yourselves! The entire Rebel army is coming this way!" With Davis's and now Sheridan's men in a state of irretrievable panic, other units around them began to flee to the rear, directly toward Rosecrans's headquarters.

The only unit in the area to stand fast was quickly enveloped on three sides. The situation was hopeless, so its commander, Brigadier General William H. Lytle, who had been a lawyer and author before the war and a hard fighter during it, ordered a desperate last gasp charge into the enemy lines to his unit's front. Lytle cried out, "All right men, we can die but once. This is the time and place. Let us charge!" As the Union line moved out, its general was shot in the spine, but he still rode forward until three more bullets blew him from his saddle. He died shortly after. With their popular commander dead, Lytle's men fled rearward as best they could, with the survivors joining the other Union formations surging backward.

One of the men in Rosecrans's headquarters was a man sent by President Lincoln to observe the Tennessee theater: Assistant Secretary of War Charles Dana. Dana kept notes on the battle and wrote extensively on his war experiences after the conflict. He had been awake for almost two days and had just about fallen asleep in the grass when he was awakened by the sound of Longstreet's attack starting. After he collected himself, he rose and saw a disturbing sight: General Rosecrans on his knees, crossing himself. Dana realized that if Rosecrans was doing that openly, the situation must be dire. And it was. Dana got on his horse and looked about. He then witnessed the collapse of the Union right flank firsthand.

Near Dana, Rosecrans assembled as many of his staff as he could and told them, "If you care to live any longer, get away from here." Then, according to Dana, "the entire headquarters around me disappeared. The graybacks [Southern soldiers] came through in a rush, and soon the musket balls and cannon shot reached the place where Rosecrans had just recently stood. The whole right of the army had apparently been routed."

Naturally, the Confederates were ecstatic (at least its generals, especially Longstreet, who has been in command of the breakthrough). A nearby Rebel cannoneer heard Longstreet exclaim, "They have fought their last man, and *he* is running." General Bragg had called on his generals to push the Union right into McLemore's Cove and destroy it, but this was better—the entire Union right had disappeared. Now the key was to pivot his troops from his left around like a swinging door and move them north to destroy the Union general from Virginia: George Henry Thomas.

As for Rosecrans and the rest of the Union right, they fled toward Chattanooga through a narrow gap in the formidable Missionary Ridge behind the Union lines. There, a group of journalists took note of how "men, animals, vehicles became a mass of struggling, cursing, shouting, frightened life." The headlong rush through the gap eventually became a clogged 1863 version of a traffic jam. Luckily for these men, the Rebels attacked north toward Thomas and not them.

In the chaos, General Rosecrans, along with his chief aide, James A. Garfield, tried to salvage what he could of the situation and reach General Sheridan, perhaps in the hope of forming a Union line a bit to the rear. But as he did so, Rosecrans, Garfield, and the men around them came under intense cannon and rifle fire, preventing them from reaching Sheridan. Rosecrans and Garfield then tried to take a back road toward Thomas's position, but they were blocked by the men in gray. They rode northward another five miles through the Rossville Gap. They decided to take a road they knew would lead to Thomas, but at that moment, as they rested their horses and listened, they could hear no fighting. The men dismounted and put their heads to the ground, but they could only hear the occasional fire in the distance. They asked Union stragglers for information, but they had little to tell except that they believed the entire army was in retreat. Some soldiers from Negley's brigade told them that their unit had been shot to pieces.

At hearing this, Rosecrans began to lose himself. If Negley's unit had been destroyed, that meant that Thomas's flank had been breached and that the fighting had likely ended in a Confederate victory on that part of the battlefield too. Despite that, Rosecrans decided he would ride to Thomas's last known position and see if he could rally the men. Garfield was to ride back to Chattanooga to begin organizing the defense of the city. Garfield did the right thing and reminded Rosecrans that he was the army commander and that his place was organizing Chattanooga's defense. He should put himself at risk in an unknown situation. Garfield would go in his place. At 4 p.m., a few hours later, Rosecrans arrived in Chattanooga, his legs too tired to let him dismount his horse without help.

Garfield would arrive at Thomas's headquarters at 4 p.m. as well. The ride was dangerous. Garfield's two orderlies had been killed, and Garfield himself had been seriously wounded. "Garfield's Ride" would be the heroic action that would propel him into the presidency in 1880 (he would be assassinated a little over six months after his inauguration by a disgruntled man who had been denied a government position). Garfield was also the one who birthed the legend of General Thomas. Garfield had a message telegraphed to

Chattanooga, saying Thomas "was standing like a rock." That information was picked up by every newspaper in the Union even before word of the defeat at Chickamauga was reported. From then on, General Thomas would be known as the "Rock of Chickamauga."

Through the late afternoon and early evening, repeated Confederate attacks had pushed Thomas's line back into the horseshoe shape that gave his position its name, at least for the Union soldiers on it: "Horseshoe Ridge" (formerly known as "Snodgrass Hill"). Despite repeated Confederate attacks on three sides, which pushed them into a narrower and narrower position, Thomas's men did hold fast. A monument honoring them stands at Horseshoe Ridge today.

Chickamauga Snodgrass Hill

Gary Todd from Xinzheng, China, CC0, via Wikimedia Commons
https://commons.wikimedia.org/wiki/File:Chickamauga_Snodgrass_Hill_(10494286314).jpg

With the news from Garfield, Thomas was sure there was no possibility of a Union counterattack to relieve him. So, he set about creating a plan to extricate his men from the ever-tightening Confederate ring. Starting at dusk, each unit was to move out in line starting from the southernmost unit, which was commanded by General Reynolds. Each unit was to move to the rear of the one to its left, which would cover it as it left. They headed for McFarland's Gap and Chattanooga.

At 5:30, just as Reynolds's division was about to move out, it was hit by a strong Confederate attack led by St. John Liddell. This attack came so suddenly and with such ferocity that it threatened to break through Reynolds's line and enter Thomas's defensive ring. If that happened, all the men with Thomas would be killed or captured. General Thomas himself took command of one of Reynolds's brigades, and just as they were about to break, he rallied them and told them to charge: "There they are! Clear them out!" The Union men did just that, pushing the Rebel unit to the rear and taking two hundred prisoners. They then rejoined Reynolds's lines and began to move to the rear.

In almost total darkness, three Union formations remained: the 21st and 22nd Ohio and the 22nd Michigan. They had been fighting almost all day and night, and they were asked to cover the retreat. Union General Brannan called to nearby General George Gordon Granger, "The enemy are forming for another assault; we have not another round of ammunition—what should we do?" Granger replied, "Fix bayonets and go for them." Down the remaining Union line, the dreaded command "Fix bayonets!" rang out. Soon, the Union charge was moving forward, and the men actually pushed the Confederates back a bit before they realized the Northerners were out of ammunition. Soon, the Rebel units surrounded the charging Union men. From those three valiant regiments, over three hundred men were killed and wounded, and over five hundred were taken prisoner.

Still, this sacrifice and the skill with which the retreat was carried out saved the Union's left wing under Thomas. The Union men disappeared so well that many Southern units were unaware they were gone and actually began firing on their own men, many of whom were in positions that had just been occupied by the North.

General Longstreet was irritated that Thomas had slipped away, but his men were elated—they had won a great victory. As he retreated, one Federal lieutenant, the future writer Ambrose Bierce, recollected that he heard the Rebel yell as he retreated. "It was the ugliest sound that any mortal ever heard—even a mortal exhausted and unnerved by two days of hard fighting, without sleep, without rest, without food and without hope." Along the line of the Federal retreat were many wounded who were too hurt and exhausted to go on. They simply laid down on the side of the road and waited to die.

Thomas collected as many men for a defense at Rossville as he could in case the Rebels were hard on their heels, but they were not. In yet another misstep, Braxton Bragg could not be convinced that he had won a great victory, even though his generals and staff told him so. They encouraged him to reorganize his forces and press the Union back to Chattanooga before they had time to organize a defense, but he was not convinced, and he would not be moved. His officers even brought up a Confederate private who had witnessed the Union retreat to tell Bragg that the Union was fleeing in disarray. Bragg still would not believe it. He asked the soldiers, "Do you even know what a retreat looks like?" The soldier, not caring who he was talking to after days of fighting, simply said, "I ought to, General; I've been fighting with you during your whole campaign."

During the war, in the years after, and in the history books since, Bragg has been chided for not following up on his victory. Some say that his losses were so severe in both men and horses that the Confederate Army in Tennessee was in no condition to continue the fight. Others say that the Union was in worse shape, having sustained heavy losses as well as a demoralizing defeat, and that, at the very least, Bragg should have moved toward Chattanooga. Bragg's generals were angry, and Longstreet was critical of him from that moment until the day he died. Cavalry commander Nathan Bedford Forrest soon separated his command from Bragg after threatening his commander's life. D. H. Hill was a personal enemy until the day he died, as were others.

Bragg decided to move onto Missionary Ridge, where he could observe the many routes into Chattanooga and send out scouts for more information. He believed that Rosecrans was too far for immediate relief and supply and that he would slowly grind the Union position into submission and retake the city. This never happened. Though Rosecrans was removed from command shortly thereafter, he and the Union forces in the city quickly reorganized and slowly built up their strength, not the other way around. Soon, they would move out of the Chattanooga area and push the enemy back into Georgia at the Battle of Missionary Ridge, which happened two months later at the end of November.

Conclusion

The Battle of Chickamauga, the second-most bloodiest battle of the American Civil War, is largely forgotten today. Since it came so soon after what many people realized at the time was a turning point at Gettysburg, the battle was seen by the Southerners as a wasted opportunity to recapture Chattanooga and perhaps recapture much of Tennessee. For the Union, the loss of life was tragic, and General Rosecrans's career was over. However, the Union defeat was only temporary. After Missionary Ridge, they drove the Confederates off the Chickamauga battlefield and pushed them back even farther.

Still, the idea that Tennessee was lost was a hard one for the South to bear. Tennessee was important not only for resources but also as a conduit between the Confederate West and East, as well as an important member of the secession. Additionally, fighting in Tennessee would prevent the Union from driving through Georgia to the Atlantic coast, cutting the Confederacy in half in the East.

In December 1864, the Confederacy appointed recovered General John Bell Hood to attack central Tennessee to hopefully force the Union drive under Sherman in Georgia to halt. Hood's reckless aggression at the Battles of Nashville and Franklin, with the latter being a particularly bloody affair, probably sped the Southern collapse rather than slowed it. Hood lost men in reckless attacks that could have been better deployed in defense.

Today, Gettysburg, Vicksburg, Chancellorsville, and a whole host of other battles are remembered more than Chickamauga, but the men who fought and died there should be remembered in the same way as the veterans from those other more famous battles.

Here's another book by Captivating History that you might like

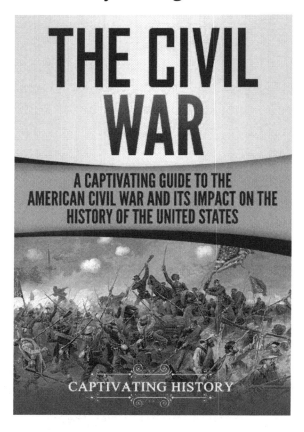

Free Bonus from Captivating History (Available for a Limited time)

Hi History Lovers!

Now you have a chance to join our exclusive history list so you can get your first history ebook for free as well as discounts and a potential to get more history books for free! Simply visit the link below to join.

Captivatinghistory.com/ebook

Also, make sure to follow us on Facebook, Twitter and Youtube by searching for Captivating History.

Bibliography

"Chickamauga." American Battlefield Trust.
https://www.battlefields.org/learn/civil-war/battles/chickamauga

"Civil War Weapons." Civil War Academy. Last modified July 21, 2020. https://www.civilwaracademy.com/civil-war-weapons

THE CIVIL WAR. Directed by Ken Burns. PBS, September 1990.

Foote, Shelby. THE CIVIL WAR: A NARRATIVE. FREDERICKSBURG TO MERIDIAN. New York: Vintage, 1986.

"Life of the Civil War Soldier in the Army." American Battlefield Trust. Last modified March 26, 2021.
https://www.battlefields.org/learn/articles/life-civil-war-soldier-army

McPherson, James M. BATTLE CRY OF FREEDOM: THE CIVIL WAR ERA. New York: Oxford University Press, 2003.

Made in United States
Orlando, FL
18 June 2023

34257642R00041